I Once Knew an Indian Woman

by May Ebbitt Cutler

new edition edited by Keir Cutler

first published in 1967.
new edition copyright 2020.
All rights belonging to Keir Cutler.
www.keircutler.com

ISBN: 978-1-7770655-0-8 (book)
ISBN: 978-1-7770655-1-5 (ebook)

Editor's note:

My mother, May Ebbitt Cutler, (1923-2011), was a truly remarkable person. She was the founder of Tundra Books, a publishing house which she ran for 28 years. She was the first female mayor of Westmount, Quebec, and chosen by the Montreal *Gazette* in the year 2000 as one of the "Top 100 Montrealers in History."

In 1967 she self-published her childhood memoir. Different titles were considered before it emerged as *I Once Knew an Indian Woman*. Awarded first prize in the Canadian Centennial Literary Competition, the book received rave reviews. The now-defunct *Ottawa Journal* said the work ought to become "a small classic" and urged its readers to get the book and live in "the spell of a memorable tale." The *Calgary Herald* praised it as "an exquisite little gem." When it was published in the United States in 1973, the *New York Times* review stated, "Simplicity isn't easy to find any more and neither is goodness. . . . Madame Dey is a marvellous figure. Her story is revealed gently, almost unobtrusively. . . . A story like this is almost impossible to tell without cuteness or sentimentality. [May] Ebbitt Cutler has managed it." The *New York Times Book Review* picked *I Once Knew an Indian Woman* as "an outstanding book of the year."

My mother and I went back to Mont-Tremblant, Quebec, where the book is set, not long before her death. She showed me the various locations that she so vividly described. We discussed my performing her award-winning work as a monologue and what changes she might make to the story to update it for the current century. This new edition is the result.

My mother died in 2011 at the age of 87. She spent her final days in the oncology ward of the old Royal Victoria Hospital in Montreal. Towards the end, she had lost much of her memory due to a spreading cancer. I spent time reading to her various classics that she had enjoyed through her long life. One of them was "a small classic" — her book — about her childhood summers in the Laurentians. A childhood, which due to her illness, she no longer remembered.

Is it a true story? The short answer is I don't know. Novelist Guillermo Erades says that "all true stories are fiction," since telling a story involves a subjective selection of events. In the case of *I Once Knew an Indian Woman*, my mother was writing about what she had been an eyewitness to thirty years earlier as a child. She wrote entirely from memory. Her three main characters are known only by nicknames, "the King," "the curé" and "Madame Dey" ("Dey" representing the letter "D" in French). Consequently, it may be more accurate to say that all true stories are based on truly believed stories, which are in turn based on notoriously inaccurate memories and the desire to tell a good tale. Whatever the case, my mother did witness something that haunted her for decades afterwards as "an insistent truth." Whether truth or legend, *I Once Knew an Indian Woman* is a story that once heard is never forgotten.

Keir Cutler, 2020.

I Once Knew an Indian Woman

Not being the offspring of a family with any claim to distinction, not coming from a background I felt any need to live up to, or live down, I have always been impatient with those who express emotional attachment to the past. People might not yet be perfect, but it suited me to think we were better than we had ever been. The belief that we were once wiser and kinder, more courageous and more beautiful, that we once had instinctive understanding we have lost, I dismissed as sentimental myth.

And yet I had no right to such an attitude, for I once knew a woman who was living proof of the validity of that belief. Perhaps because middle-age is upon me (how painful it is to admit it like this in print) and I recognize that more of my life now lies behind me than is likely to extend ahead, I can face other realities, which until now the arrogance of youth helped me to ignore, and at last tell this story that has nagged at me like a suppressed but highly insistent truth all these years.

The aboriginal woman I write about, Madame Dey, does not fit sociological theories we use to classify our native peoples. Not only did she survive in the 20th century by her ancient skills and values, but she shamed that world, showing up the hollowness of many of its most dearly held pretensions about itself.

Perhaps only the eyes of the child that I was could have discerned her greatness and yet, as I bring my present awareness to re-examine that old evidence, her dimensions have grown, until now, out of all the summers of my childhood, she emerges to stand in the foreground.

I was taken to the Laurentian village where she lived for the first of my remembered summers in 1927. The old village of Mont-Tremblant, known back then by the lake it lay beside, Lac Mercier, was less than a hundred miles north of Montreal. The area seemed very remote because of the dusty four-hour train trip during which I slithered restlessly about on the varnished rattan seats while my mother gave me oranges to peel, pointed out the engine pulling us each time the train went round a turn, and warned me to "sit small" when the conductor passed to collect the tickets.

The lake was shaped like a boomerang, two miles long with the Canadian Pacific Railroad tracks edging the outer rim, the railway station and village snuggling at the curve. The dirt road into the village followed the tracks as far as the station, then swerved sharply away to continue on to "the big lake," Lac Tremblant, three miles further. As I try to describe it, I see that the lake and road really resembled *two* boomerangs placed back to back.

The village did not differ importantly from others in the Laurentians where Montrealers were already building summer cottages or vacationing in clapboard hotels. It offered only one diversion by which one could tick off the passing of the summer days. Each evening the summer people and a few of the villagers gathered on the platform of the railway station to watch the arrival of the Montreal train, then moved leisurely up to the general store a few yards away to await the sorting of the mail. Sundays divided the weeks as fathers came from town and the tiny Roman Catholic church rang its bell at hourly intervals all morning to summon the faithful to mass. In those first years, before the big white structure that still dominates the lake was built, the church was too small to hold everyone; and the hill behind it was crowded with hatted, high-heeled girls who climbed gingerly up the slope, helped by their coated escorts, so they could see, as well as hear, the service through the open windows.

Being of Irish Protestant parents I never attended services, but since the cottage we rented every summer for a decade was next door to the church, I was often in it. The door was always open. If I was around when the priest rang the bell with reasonable accuracy at six o'clock mornings and evenings, he would let me "help" him pull the thick, rough rope. If I was around, as I had no right to be, at other times when he was not there, I would pump at a pedal of the organ in the balcony until I finally extracted a booming note that would draw my mother's attention to my absence and bring her running.

The thirty French-Canadian families that lived in the village the year round, many in unpainted, weather-greyed boxes on stilts, eked out a marginal living. They had small vegetable gardens, every inch of which had been cleared by hand from the rocky mountain slopes. A few had cows from which we got our milk "still warm." My mother, having grown up on a farm in central Ireland, was delighted by its natural state; she remarked repeatedly on its wholesomeness and flavour, which she believed were spoiled in the pasteurized milk sold in the city. "They take all the goodness out of it," she often would say. Also, being unseparated, the milk needed only to stand awhile in the icebox to acquire a top layer of cream thick enough for whipping.

Serving the summer people was, of course, the main employment of the villagers. They worked the hotels, did small carpentry jobs, scraped the dirt roads, cut ice from the lake for the sawdust-filled ice-sheds, took in laundry, sent their daughters to work in the houses of the better-off vacationers and sent all their children to pick and sell the wild strawberries, raspberries and blueberries that consecutively seemed to last the summer. Downhill skiing had not yet opened the Laurentians to winter activity, so the men went off to the lumber camps in November to send home the fifteen dollars a month by which their families survived between summers.

Life had not always been quite so hard for them. An industry had provided more regular employment, but it had closed down the year before our arrival. Known only as "the chemical plant," it had extracted chemicals from wood, and bits of charcoal were strewn everywhere like pebbles. For many years rumours persisted that it would reopen, but it never did, and its vast sheds and ovens became irresistible to all of us children. Each afternoon terminated with the kind of ritual play that distinguishes children from adults and makes a youngster glad he has not yet crossed the dividing line, as we (yes, we, for even I managed occasionally to escape my mother's watchfulness on the pretext of going to the general store) flung chunks of charcoal high up the sloping tin roofs. We listened as long as we dared to their bumpy trip back down, then ran to hide in the nearby woods before the only Englishman who lived year-round in the village (and had, naturally, been left in charge of things by the departed English management) came out of his house on the other side of the creek and shouted threateningly at us. Gradually, through the years, his interest lapsed (perhaps his stipend for looking after the property also decreased); he went on to chicken farming while the shed disappeared, board by board, and the tin, sheet by sheet, to repair the houses of the villagers. Deprived of the climax of their drama, the children gathered there less and less.

After the plant shut down, the company houses were leased out to villagers. The imposing hilltop residence of the former manager went to the parish priest for an unstated rental, while the oldest house, a two-storey unpainted box that had been vertically divided down the middle to shelter two families, went to Madame Dey for two dollars a month. Unpretentious as her house was, its location on a smaller hill just behind the station gave it a commanding view of the village and lake, and blocked the otherwise uninterrupted view from the priest's house behind it. The two properties met in a small valley between the two hills where the vegetable garden and outhouse of the one bordered on the expansive, well-kept lawn of the other.

The three of them — the priest, the Englishman and Madame Dey — formed a triangle of competing power in the village. The priest, known always as "Monsieur le Curé," was a thin, ascetic, bespectacled man who, it was said, had been intended for higher posts in the church, but because of a lung ailment, had been assigned to this little Laurentian parish where the high altitude would have a salutary effect on his health, and the small size of the congregation a not-too-serious drain on his limited energy. The Englishman was known as "the King" (the English word was used mockingly and never translated into "le Roi"). The implied status of the title seemed to please him more than the sarcasm annoyed him. And finally, Madame Dey, the native; her name came from her deceased French-Canadian husband's last name, which began with the letter "D", in French pronounced "Dey."

In a way, I suppose, they resembled the triple forces that formed Canada itself: the religion of the French, the economic strength of the English, and the prior and continuing existence of the indigenous peoples. But while "le Curé" and "the King" had establishments of considerable dimensions behind their power, Madame Dey exercised hers by personality alone — not that I wish to imply the other two were at all deficient in that sphere. Although I could not have given so sophisticated an analysis of the three of them during my childhood, I do not think I was ever so young as not to recognize the reality of their positions.

In the end, just as it happened in Canada itself, Madame Dey was ousted from her home and forced to live on the outskirts of the village in the only vacant house she could find. But that happened after the main events of this story, and I mention it here just to orient the reader who likes the broader politics, economics and geography clarified before he can relax and concentrate on details.

My mother was the only person I ever knew to be on friendly speaking terms with all three. She was a lonely woman between my father's weekend visits. Although she was acquainted with other summer people, she felt more at home with the villagers, perhaps because their lives resembled more closely her own early farm life. She knew no French beyond a few adjectives to describe the weather like *beau* and *trempe*. Few of the villagers spoke English, but she welcomed small pretexts to visit them, such as purchasing a few stalks of rhubarb here or a head of leaf lettuce there, and she communicated in an elaborate pantomime, accompanying the gestures with unarticulated English nouns. She knew all of their names, could disentangle the complex family relationships of all the Tremblays and Sequins, and — thanks to Madame Dey — knew all of the gossip concerning them.

Her friendliness to the priest was at first confined to inquiries about his health and the financial success of the annual tombola, and had a deliberateness to it. She might be Orange Irish, but "one must not be bigoted," as she liked to point out to my father, who felt no similar obligation. As the priest passed our house going to and from church, she would call out to him: "And how are you feelin' today, *missyew*?" (her rejection of bigotry never extended quite so far as to call him "father," and "Monsieur le Curé" seemed more French than she could manage). He would reply in his gracious, slightly formal, English with an odd little smile, which I now think was occasioned by my mother's resemblance in both appearance and speech to the stereotype of the hearty Irishwoman. Often he would turn his attention immediately to me to inquire after the state of health of the doll I always seemed to have with me. My mother was convinced that his faltering health was caused by his "having to drink all that wine Sunday mornings without so much as a mouthful of food in his stomach," but it was some years before she presumed on her acquaintance with him sufficiently to "have a little chat" with his housekeeper and suggest he be coaxed into taking "at least a bit of eggnog each mornin' to coat the stomach."

I thought he was quite the nicest man imaginable (perhaps because he always noticed my presence by speaking to me). I loved the drama that his tall lean figure, further elongated by his cassock, engendered as he walked by, his skirts flapping a little cloud of dust around him. He was, I realize now, the first intellectual I ever met, and both his strength and weakness as a priest perhaps derived from that. If the size of the congregation did not strain his energy, its poverty and backwardness did. But, like many intellectuals, he was not at his best in moments of great private tragedy that strike nearly all families at one time or another. The display of uncontrolled emotion seemed to embarrass him. As required by his calling, he attended the deathbeds and officiated at the funerals, but he kept such contacts to the minimum. Much as they appreciated his efforts on their behalf, his parishioners never quite felt he was one of them.

The King, on the other hand, never was and never wanted to be identified in any way with the villagers. He was English-English, as distinguished from Canadian-English. I have long forgotten what part of England he came from, but some of his idioms fascinated me: he always *knowed* or *knewed* everything. A ruddy-faced man with a reddish-grey barbershop quartet moustache, he walked with his thumbs inserted under his suspenders. Stretched to their limit over a humpty-dumpty stomach, they held his trouser legs well above the ankle. He cowed his wife, a tiny, tight-lipped woman who crocheted lace tablecloths and doilies with compulsive ferocity. She never spoke a word in his presence and never stopped talking outside of it. Her occasional visits to our cottage were not welcomed with much enthusiasm by my mother, who claimed "I can never get a word in edgewise with that woman." Not that my mother got many words in edgewise or otherwise with the King, but I think she was flattered that he seemed to like to talk to her.

Besides being rent collector and caretaker for the departed chemical company, he looked after "things" for those summer people who rented out their cottages when they were not using them. That is not to imply he repaired anything; merely that he received complaints, which he transmitted to the owners. The cottage we rented was one of these. My mother's first visits to his house, which lay at the other end of the village beyond the station and general store, were instigated by a leak in the woodshed roof and the running dry of the well. We saw him more frequently after she decided to buy her weekend chickens from him because "at least he kills them dead." During our first summers she had bought them from the farmer who delivered our fresh warm milk, but this terminated one Saturday morning when she opened the newspaper-wrapped parcel and found the chicken to be still alive — not what one would call lively, but alive none-theless. As she had told my father later, she'd had "the very devil of a time killing it." Even after she beheaded it out-side on the grass with an axe, its legs waved at her re-proachfully. She was far from being squeamish, but a chicken that would not die posed metaphysical problems that a woman in a hurry to get a bird plucked, cleaned out, stuffed and into the oven has neither the time nor the desire to ponder.

The King refused to take advance orders and did not deliver his chickens. He was known as a penny pincher, and the neighbouring children kept out of his way, for they did not seem to feel that the *noblesse oblige* he displayed in asking them to run messages made up for the lack of more tangible remuneration. On Friday afternoons when we appeared, he would lead us grandly up to his pullet houses, ask my mother which particular bird she fancied, and with impres-sive efficacy, catch it, string it up by the legs and kill it on the spot with a special hooked knife. I was never quite cer-tain that it was the exact chicken she had selected from the great-feathered clucking flock, but the King was, and my mother never challenged his choice. I realize now that he possessed something that can silence superfluous quibbling in most adults and absolutely overawe children: style.

I would watch these killings, waiting for the moment of stillness, with shivery, but unquestioning, fascination. It was not until some years later, when I recounted to a city school friend how I had seen many chickens killed and was looked at with horror, that I felt I must have been deficient in some basic decency to have stood by and willingly witnessed such bloody scenes.

Carrying the dead chicken like a trophy, the King would then lead us down the hill to his house. Its living room impressed me with its elaborate furnishings in contrast to the utilitarian modesty of the summer cottages and the austerity of the villagers' houses where all living, other than sleeping, went on in the kitchen. He would order his wife to wrap the chicken, seat himself in a gigantic black leather-covered easy chair beside a lace-covered table, motion my mother to a straight-backed dining room chair, pick up one of the farm papers he subscribed to and bring us up to date on the state of chicken farming. I don't think my mother, in spite of her farm background, understood these reports on feed mixtures, breeds and egg wholesaling any more than I did, but she made appropriate interjections and, as soon as she could do so politely, turned the conversation to what both she and I never tired of hearing: his stories of the Great War. Meanwhile, the chicken duly wrapped, his wife would take her place on another dining room chair next to the piano that was never played and silently crochet, rather, I realize now, like a suspicious and disapproving chaperon.

He had been a sergeant during the war — was ever man more suited to the job? — and his stories of life in the trenches of France made that muddy miserable world more real to me than all the accounts, photographs and films I have seen since. He had been wounded by shrapnel on his left side, and his hand often moved there to massage it gently as he talked. Neither the ribbons and medals framed above the piano, nor the numerous photographs of him in breeches hanging on the other walls, dramatized his involvement as did those movements of his hand. "I'm just a hollow shell inside," he once said proudly. "They cut out everything. The last time the doctor came at me with the knife, he said: 'That's it, soldier. It's no use coming back here.'" His stomach became for me a mystery to contemplate, like a vast, empty cave; I was eye level with it for much of this story, and when he stood up, his suspenders stretched up the long slope to his head like tracks over a mountain.

In some ways he fancied himself the English gentleman. His war pension made him independent; his chicken farming was carried on with the scientific, but enthusiastic, precision of the English amateur who can pursue a hobby the more ardently the less he depends on it for a livelihood. That is how I see him now. As a child, standing beside my mother or sitting on the hassock that he would nudge towards me with his foot. I saw him as Old Kaspar in Southey's poem *The Battle Blenheim* and myself as little

Wilhelmine looking up "with wonder-waiting eyes" and asking: "Now tell us all about the war, And what they fought each other for." I knew many lines of that poem, for my father, a quiet, watery-eyed Irishman whom my mother seemed forever to be waking from a dream, would often recite it aloud to himself. He was tone-deaf, and declaimed poetry as others sing songs; his preference, with the exception of the Psalms, was for verse with a strong storyline and a military setting. High among his favourites were Felicia Hemans' *Casablanca* ("The boy stood on the burning deck, Whence all but he had fled;") and Charles Wolfe's *The Burial of Sir John Moore after Corunna* ("Slowly and sadly we laid him down, From the field of his fame fresh and gory; We carved not a line, and we raised not a stone, But left him alone with his glory."). Oddly English for an Irishman? My father's ancestors had come to Ireland with Cromwell, and he had come to Canada, he said, "because I wanted to die as I was born, under the Union Jack." His wish came true by a narrow margin: he died the year before Canada adopted its own flag. But I must not spend time talking about him here, for he plays little role in this summer story. Unlike my mother, he was not sociable, and on weekends after meals (during which he was a captive audience for her reports on the week's events) he would sit in the sun in the garden to doze and perhaps to dream of those old heroics on which his youth had been fed. I found it odd then, though I no longer do, that he took little interest in the King's realistic accounts of an actual battlefield: the romance of wars increases the greater one's distance from them.

Like the children sitting at Old Kaspar's feet, I never did find out what the "war to end all wars" was all about, and to this day I am not too sure I know. However, in those days when we had neither television nor radio and very few books, the stories told by the King were very important to me. He was the best storyteller I knew with one exception.

That exception was Madame Dey, and it was her house we visited almost daily through a decade of summers.

My mother's meeting with her was auspicious. I don't know if I was really present on the occasion, or if I just think I was because my mother described it so often to so many people (she seemed to feel she had to justify her friendship with Madame Dey). It was our first summer there and I had developed a feverish cold, which my mother believed would only respond if my chest were treated to a rub of camphorated oil. She was asking for it in the general store without success when a deep booming voice came at her from behind in English: "Pardon me, madam, but I know where you can get camphorated oil." My mother turned and there stood Madame Dey: a giant of a woman in a Mother Hubbard skirt with men's socks and shoes (her huge feet could be contained in nothing less), short, straight black hair clipped tightly to the side of her head with a bobby pin, great black half-moon eyes reaching out over high cheekbones and a powerful jaw ready to take on all comers. Not one to be put off by physical appearances as long as a friendly voice accompanied them, my mother later confessed that on this occasion she was quite taken aback. "'Twas as if she'd come out of the *airth*."

Madame Dey had picked some wild ginger only that morning that could soothe an upset stomach when boiled in a tea (much more effective than camphorated oil). We soon learned she had a wide assortment of home remedies, all of them at least as effective as anything sold in the general store.

The friendship that developed between the two women was based on more than gratitude on my mother's side: she had discovered the only woman villager who could speak English. Madame Dey actually spoke better English than she spoke French. She had learned it working as a servant in upper middle class English homes of Westmount, Quebec, whereas her French, learned first from her husband and not much enriched by the French-Canadian labourers and farmers among whom she lived, remained on the patois level or, as it is now called, *joual*. Her first language was Mohawk. Since Madame Dey's house was the oldest building in the village, its strategic location was understandable enough. So was its appearance. Its unpainted wood had mellowed during the thirty or forty years it had been washed by rain and snow until its deep grey appeared black from the distance and the black was further emphasized by the white-painted trim on the door and window frames where rot tends to attack. Its two storeys had been divided down the centre between two front doors leading into the respective dwelling units. It was possible to go from one to the other without going outside. A doorway had been broken through between the two all-purpose kitchens that took up the ground floor, but Madame Dey kept it closed all day in summer. She made her living by doing laundry for the summer people who had "homes" (as distinct from the "cottages" in our village) at the big lake up the road. In the right-hand kitchen her vast wood stove burned all day long to keep the oval tubs of sheets boiling and her collection of irons warm. The ironing itself she did in the cooler left-hand kitchen, carrying the irons back and forth by the outside entrances. These detours into the open air not only served to cool her off, but provided a view of everything going on around the general store and train station, and of nearly the whole expanse of the lake. Her shout of greeting or inquiry to any villager who passed on foot or wagon was one of the most familiar sounds in the area, welcome to some, like my mother, and embarrassing to others.

The King particularly resented her inclusion of him in this indiscriminate camaraderie. He referred to her contemptuously as "Mrs. In-One-Door-And-Out-The-Other." I suspect that the detours he often made across the creek and through the chemical company grounds to get from one side of the village to the other were motivated more by a desire to avoid her shouts than the need to keep an eye on his obligations. Although she always shouted to him in English, her questions of "How are the chickens today?" or "Is there going to be another war?" reduced him to the level of the villagers, a de-classing he hated and which she, with her infallible instinct for recognizing pretentiousness, pursued with amusement. She believed he would, if he could, have her evicted from her perch, but in those early years she was confident that the promise of protection given her by the departed company manager's wife would keep her safe. Nonetheless she was always careful to get her rent in on time, telling her foster daughter who was sent with the two dollars, not to surrender it unless the King was home and gave a receipt.

My mother and I would never go to the general store without dropping in (or up) to see Madame Dey. Evenings, my mother would often wait there while I went to the post office to get the mail, then stay on reading tidbits from the *Montreal Star* by the light of an oil lamp which Madame Dey removed from its nail on the wall and placed on a table for the purpose. Her big hands moving incessantly over her knitting, Madame Dey would sit listening avidly to my mother's very personal selection of crime news from page three (to which my mother added editorial comments by way of sighs and tut-tutting, and rhetorical questions about what the world was coming to). Only when my mother would glance in shocked surprise at the clock, declare determinedly, "The child must be got to bed," and start to fold the paper, would Madame Dey interrupt to inquire pleasingly: "Do they say anything about California in there, Madam?" My mother would shake her head and promise to search the paper more carefully the following day. Even when she found California datelines, she refused to report them to Madame Dey, who, she believed, was already worried enough about her youngest son with hearing of "the goings on of those wild actresses."

According to his mother, Gene was the handsomest and cleverest of her four sons; since the other sons, all of whom were married and lived in the village, were certainly good looking, he must have been quite striking. We never met him, but we did see him once in the distance, running down the path from her house to a convertible where a blond woman sat waiting. He was wearing plus-fours, which in those days we associated with the Prince of Wales and the international set. In the village we saw that rich, distant, dissolute world as only a cloud of dust left by the big open touring cars and roadsters that sped back and forth from the expensive, elegant hotels at the big lake. Gene had been working as a bellhop at the hotel that stood on a cliff overlooking the big lake when he met the woman. Whether she was widowed or divorced I was never told, but she was fifteen years older than Gene, and when she invited him to go back to California with her as her "chauffeur," he accepted. I could not understand in those days why Madame Dey was so upset over the arrangement; it seemed to me she ought to have been proud that Gene had been given such an opportunity to advance himself. But I now realize that Madame Dey understood precisely the implications of the arrangement; and while she might be helpless to stop it, she would not be cajoled into pretending to approve. For the first few years after he left, letters came from Gene's "employer" every few months, then they dropped to one a year and, finally, stopped altogether. Madame Dey would always carry the last one received in her bosom, and would ask my mother to read it over to her from time to time, as if she hoped to understand more in each rereading. There was certainly little information in them ("Gene is fine and sends his love. Perhaps we will get east this summer, and he will be able to visit you"). They were written in what my mother called "a fine hand" on tinted stationery, with the woman's name and address engraved on both the notepaper and lined envelopes. Gene himself never wrote. He had gone to the village school longer than her other children, but the six grades taught in one room (where most of the teacher's energy, it was said, went to keep discipline) never seemed to have prepared anyone to do more than write his name and recite his catechism.

At least once each summer, my mother would bring her own pad and pen over to Madame Dey's to write a reply on her behalf. Each letter ended with the same words: "Madame Dey wants you to send Gene home."

Because of the laundry, Madame Dey's house — both sides of it — always smelled of javel water and starch. Behind the structure was a garden full of vegetables and, by late summer each year, soaring sunflowers. Madame Dey loved sunflowers, her native ancestors sprinkled sunflower seeds on top of the graves of the dead to sustain them in their long journey to the afterlife. Just beyond the garden, long clotheslines of sheets and shirts waved snappingly. The thin French-Canadian man from the city who ran the post office and general store as if it were a short-staffed military head-quarters under perpetual siege had little time for pleas-antries. (The stacks of bill-books of accounts owing him, filed alphabetically behind the counter, could not have reas-sured him much that the siege would ever let up.) But he seemed to start each day optimistically, and for those cus-tomers who appeared before eleven a.m. he even managed a smile and a reference to the weather; he said he could al-ways tell whether an uncertain morning would clear or not simply by looking out to see if Madame Dey had put up her wash.

Madame Dey shared the house with her married daughter, whose husband worked as a handyman for a hotel at the big lake, her daughter's baby — soon to be added to annually – – and a little girl of my age with long black pigtails and pretty name: Amande? Yolande? Fernande? (how odd that I should have forgotten exactly when it was such a nice word to say). Amande, as I shall call her, never knew her real mother and father. She had been taken in when a few days old by Madame Dey, an act of charity my mother often referred to when she defended her against charges of being "a character." "She's a good heart, that woman," my mother would say. "It's not many as would take somebody else's baby into the house after bringing up six of her own, and her not getting a red cent for it, either."

Amande was a very quiet child whom I cannot remember ever laughing. I found this quite understandable. Would not tragedy so impenetrable as losing one's parents when one was too young to know what was happening not condition anyone forever to sadness? In those early years my French, learned on our east-end Montreal street, was restricted to words for toys, food and clothing, and to expressions essential for play such as *tiens, m'en va,* and *vas t'en.* I could not, therefore, question her about it, and my mother warded off my persistent inquiries as to how precisely a catastrophe of such magnitude could come about with "Ye're too young to understand such things" until, finally, when I was no longer too young to understand, I no longer needed to ask. Although I could sit as happily as my mother and listen to Madame Dey's stories of the human experiment based on her own life and that of others (she was already well over fifty when we met her), I was often sent out to play with

Amande while they had "grown-up" talk. Our "play" always took the form of helping out. We would bring in the split logs for Madame Dey's stove, search for carrots large enough to pull in the vegetable garden, and best of all, pick bugs off the potato plants. For this chore, Amande put a few inches of water from the garden pump into two of the tall green bleach bottles so that once the bugs were dropped in, they could not climb back out. Together we worked methodically up and down the rows of potato plants, stopping from time to time to match bottles and see who had the larger collection. Finding the lovely hard-back orange bugs, which I could not distinguish from ladybugs, and watching them drop down inside the green glass held a magic for me that no berry-picking, which it somewhat resembled, could ever match.

With the exception of her beloved Gene in California, Madame Dey's other children had children of their own and lived much as the other villagers. Only one of them, Leo, carried on his native heritage. He was a toweringly slim man who walked with sprint-like strides, raising and putting down his feet as if testing the firmness of the ground. He worked as a guide. He had the reputation of never coming back empty-handed from a fishing or hunting trip, even though most of the lakes in the area were said to be "fished out," and the partridges were already scared away by the time the trees were sufficiently bare of leaves for amateurs to sight them. The uncertainty of his income (further aggravated by his drinking) and the poverty of his family were a continual cause of worry to Madame Dey, who immediately sent the used clothing my mother gave her at the end of each summer to Leo's long-suffering wife. Despite his dislike of regular work, he still managed to build his family a house with wood and corrugated tin filched from the abandoned chemical plant. I don't know who owned the land on the frog pond, as we called it, halfway between our lake and the big lake, where he put the structure, for no one protested his right to it, but the stolen materials were another matter. By the time the King learned of this brash concentrated displacement of company property, the house was as finished as it would ever be. He visited Leo in an imperious rage and ordered its return, but he was neither prepared to accept the hammer Leo offered him, by way of answer, and dismantle it himself, nor was he willing to pay anyone else to do it. Leo only laughed off his threats to call the provincial police, for he knew that not even the King would dare to intrude such an outside force into the self-regulating life of the village. There was a provincial police office in a town ten miles away, but I know of no occasion, not even during the emergency that is the main incident of this account, when it was ever called for help.

"Besides," as the King told my mother, rationalizing his impotence, "I never *seed* such a shack. Even the walls were covered with tin. They won't be able to live out the winter in it." Then he sniffed, his grey-red moustache moving with the contemptuous curve of his lips: "He'll go the way of his father yet. I always say if the father's no good, what can you expect of the son?"

They did, however, not only manage to pass their first winter in it but many another, and were still living there the last summer I spent at the lake. As for the references to Leo's father, it was true the son seemed to have inherited or acquired his father's intemperance, but the King's syllogism was scarcely valid since Madame Dey's other sons in the village were sober enough.

The only time I ever saw tears in Madame Dey's great black eyes was when she spoke of her late French Quebecer husband. He had died the winter before our first summer at the lake and she seemed to miss him very much, although, in my mother's view, "she was well rid of him." From the moment at the age of fifteen when she left her father's house on the Kahnawake Reserve to "run away" with Yvon, until the January morning when he was found dead in the snow, she never questioned his right to her roof and bed. He had walked out on her countless times during their marriage, leaving her to feed and shelter their children without help, and returning sometimes after as long as a year's absence without money to show for it. "But why would you take him back?" my mother would ask. I remember Madame Dey once answering, "Can the hunter help it if he must sometimes return with empty hands?"

My mother, of course, regarded Yvon's death in the snow as God's justice. She, too, could quote various proverbs and sayings, usually culled from sermons she had heard. The one she repeated most often as a kind of epitaph to the late Yvon was: "Though the mills of God grind slowly; Yet they grind exceeding small; Though with patience He stands waiting, With exactness grinds He all."

It was usually in our house, not hers, that Madame Dey talked of her husband. Perhaps loneliness brought her over for that express purpose. She would visit us a few evenings each summer (though never, of course, on weekends) if my mother had not been in to see her for a day or two. Her loud shout of "Are you in?" announced her coming long before she reached the steps of our cottage, much to my mother's mortification. In the stillness that falls over Laurentian lakes at twilight, my mother was sure the shout could be heard clear across to the far shore. Sometimes she would bring a photograph discovered on a newspaper that had previously wrapped laundry for my mother to read the caption. Always she would have in the large hidden pockets of her mountainous skirt some knitting to work on while she talked, as if having something in her hands disciplined her emotions.

She met Yvon one summer when he was working with a repair gang on the road that ran through the reserve. She had never been further than a few miles from it in her life, not even across the river to Montreal. Like many of the children on the reserve in the late 19th century, Madame Dey did not attend the government paid school run by the Roman Catholic Church. Madame Dey's parents saw the school for exactly what it was, an attempt to absorb the children into another culture, and deny their own. They kept her at home and taught her traditional skills.

When Madame Dey's father told stories of the past, so immediate were the descriptions that she assumed the Europeans had come to Canada only a few years before her birth. Madame Dey was also given to believe that the tribe would one day own everything back again, even the great evil city across the water.

At age eleven she had assisted in the delivery of a baby sister, her mother calling out the directions between spasms as matter-of-factly as if ordering the preparation of a meal.

The first non-natives she ever saw were the police who raided the reserve, barging into homes searching for liquor, enforcing Canada's Indian Act (first passed by Parliament in the year 1876), which made it a felony for natives to consume alcohol. Madame Dey's mother would sit with stony immobility waiting for the desecration to stop, then she would get up and, without a word, replace each object in its appointed place.

Since all men in Montreal were in Madame Dey's mind either policemen or drunkards, if not both, it did not seem impossible that the whole reserve might rise up some night after the city had drunk itself into a stupor and recapture it.

Yvon was not at all like the sinister intruders who raided their homes. He laughed all the time. The first French word she learned was *viens* as he held out the food to her, teasingly coaxing her toward him, holding out a sandwich from his lunch bag. "I took it and ran off like a squirrel," she told us, "and like a squirrel I went back the next day." He talked all the time in French. Soon he offered chocolate, and if she held back he would eat a piece himself to show her it was good and then proffer the rest. After two weeks, when the roadwork was finished and he said, "*Viens*," she went with him.

He took her to Montreal to live with a sister, who arranged for them to be married, and she was soon pregnant at just sixteen years of age. She accepted Yvon's drinking at first as a matter of course. Did not everyone in the evil city drink? Then, as she learned that was not so, her native loyalty sustained her. She found work as a day servant in rich English-speaking homes in Westmount, Quebec where she learned her English.

They moved to Mont-Tremblant when Yvon, during one of his resolutions to reform, took a job in the chemical factory. For ten years before his death, he was in and out of work;

and though he was frequently fired for drunkenness, he would get rehired when the factory was short-staffed. "Everyone liked him," Madame Dey said, "He was a good worker … when he worked."

Yvon's drinking increased with age. Being chronically un-employed, he started to steal things from the house to buy liquor. One extremely cold January night he had gone out drinking and come back drunk around eleven o'clock, wok-en up their adult daughter and baby grandson, then pro-ceeded to demand money from their daughter, as her hus-band's pay had arrived that day from the lumber camp where he was off working all winter. Madame Dey was awakened by her daughter's screams to find Yvon holding the baby high above his head, threatening to knock its brains out if he were not given the money.

I can still see Madame Dey the one and only time she re-counted that particular part of the story in detail, her hands tight around her knitting, her half-moon eyes staring be-yond us into the wall as if she saw it being re-enacted on a screen there. "Grandchildren are different to your own," she told us. "They're a gift. I don't remember what I said, but it scared Yvon and he put the baby down and went to bed . . . and I decided I would never allow him into the house drunk again."

The following night, returning once again intoxicated, Yvon found the doors bolted against him. Lacking either the energy or heart to make it to the barn of one of his drinking friends, he lay down to sleep in the snow, never to awake.

Often in talking about her husband, Madame Dey would put down her knitting, take a piece of neatly cut sheeting from her bosom, wipe her eyes and blow her nose, while my mother searched among her collection of reliable quotations to find one to sum it all up. If God's mills were not grinding slowly, then He was working "in a mysterious way His wonders to perform" and there was to "everything a season and a time to every purpose under heaven."

The protectiveness of the company manager's wife toward Madame Dey, and her promise that "as long as the company owned the house she would have roof over her head," arose from Madame Dey's experience in midwifery. As was the fashion the time, the manager's wife took a patronizing interest in the village families, particularly in the arrival of new children. It upset her that they should be born with just any convenient neighbour in attendance, and when she discovered Madame Dey's experience in delivering babies, she set her up as the village midwife. A pattern was established: when the wife of an employee went into labour, word was sent to the manager's wife, who in turn sent word to Madame Dey, who lived so conveniently close by. Madame Dey would gather together the bundle of clean sheets and blankets she kept ready for the purpose and answer the call. Afterwards Madame Dey would receive a fee of fifty cents for her work. The manager's wife had voluntarily set up a kind of company insurance plan covering births; her reward was to visit the new arrival later and receive the flattering gratitude of the family. Since she realized that the success of her scheme depended totally on Madame Dey's skill, she naturally had, as my mother liked to phrase it, "a soft spot in her heart for you."

Madame Dey's proprietor's interest in the affairs of all the villagers was equally understandable. Many of her shouts to the farmers who passed her house referred to their continuing fertility. But with the closing of the plant and the ending of the delivery scheme, the village women reverted to their former cooperative system and Madame Dey was less frequently called. Few babies ever seemed to arrive in summer. Indeed, I can remember only one, an eighth child born to Madame Dey's other daughter, who had married an Italian immigrant and lived near the big lake. When we visited the mother in the late afternoon to see the baby that had been born early that morning, she was already up and making supper for her family.

Much as I loved to hear Madame Dey tell about her early life and the village as it was before we arrived, what I liked most about her was something else, something I can only sum up with the word "elegance."

A strange word to apply to one so huge of body and so heavy of foot?

It was the way she did things, the care she took. She ironed cotton sheets as if they were made of silk and men's shirts as if they belonged to a lover. Remembering those neat rows of baskets along her wall with clothes flawlessly folded and waiting to be picked up. Thinking now of the machine-washed and machine-ironed clothes our laundries send back today with, as my mother would have said, "all the good taken out of them," I wonder if those women with their summer "homes" at the big lake appreciated her. Perhaps they did, for Madame Dey bragged that she never lost a customer. In spite of its sparse furnishings, even her house seemed arranged with conscious care; the rough wooden floors were almost white, for again, to use my mother's words, "they were scrubbed to the bone." Her vegetable garden was planted so neatly one would think the distance between the seeds had been measured with a ruler. Amande's white pinafores were starched like those of children in picture books; her own vast skirts, which she made from flour bags and dyed black, fell in folds as neat as a nun's. When she combed and braided Amande's hair and snapped on an elastic band to hold the ends, not a single strand hung loose. Only in the braided upswept hair of ballet dancers have I since seen such perfection.

It was strange to watch hands so large, larger even than my father's, with square-tipped fingers and tight-cropped nails, perform delicate tasks like threading a needle. Even that she did as if she were challenged to get the thread through the eye on the first try. Did she believe that the magic she performed in small household matters would somehow stretch beyond them to create orderliness in the life of her family?

Each summer, around the second or third week in August, her front doors would remain closed until evening and we would know, for she usually forewarned us, that she was away picking blueberries. She would start out around six in the morning, carrying the big empty lard pails, a lunch for herself and Amande. They would walk the three miles to the big lake and another mile into the woods where she knew the blueberries grew in quantity. Sometimes we were waiting for them when they arrived home in the late afternoon, for Madame Dey would have suggested that we stop in to get some from her. She would walk up the hill to her house, her step heavy under the weight of the pails (my mother marveled that she could lift them at all, let alone carry them so far), Amande following her, carrying two smallish pails that were used for the actual picking. Madame Dey's face would light up when she saw us. Inside she would take off her men's shoes, remove her woolen socks and put her feet into a basin of water, talking all the time triumphantly of her day. "Look at them," she would say, pointing to the pails, "not a green berry, not a leaf."

Her feet washed and dried, she would get up and pour the gauge pails slowly into assorted smaller bowls and pails, again pointing out the cleanness of her pickings as they fell, a waterfall of rolling blue marbles. I have always loved to tip a box of blueberries into a sieve for washing since then and, picking out the unripe berry, the overripe berry, a leaf or twiggy stem, remember.

She had brought her children up in her husband's religion, but except for a reproduction of the Sacred Heart on her wall (perhaps put there by one of her children), she never showed any interest in it and never attended services in the church. She ignored the curé with noticeable contempt for his youth and his avoidance of crises. "What does he under-stand?" she once said to my mother, and my mother found herself in the ironical position of defending him (a role I think she was pleased to assume) with the reply: "They say he's got a good head on his shoulders."

Kahnawake in her youth had a Catholic mission on it, but I believe she had nothing to do with it. I remember her once saying: "When you have many gods, at least you can choose among them," an interesting rejection of the tyranny of monotheism which, it seems to me now, perhaps formed the basis of her skepticism. Never short of platitudes, my mother would reassure her with only slight condescension: "You can be good if ye never went to church."

But it seemed to me that Madame Dey's memory and intelligence showed up most remarkably in, of all things, her knitting. It was a time when women wore sweaters knitted in elaborate lacy patterns of fans, flowers and leaves done, not with different coloured yarn, but by intricate increasing, decreasing, slipping and passing over of stitches. Every such sweater Madame Dey saw challenged her; she could usually analyze a design simply by looking at it. Her laundry customers often gave her their old sweaters; one night I remember her ripping out such a sweater so matted that it looked undecipherable, and memorizing the stitch backwards. My mother, who had trouble following a pattern described in a magazine or newspaper, was astonished at the feat and talked about it as we walked home that night with the beam from our flashlight bouncing ahead of us. "There's not a thing that woman can't do, except read and write."

Madame Dey was doomed, of course, doomed to be undervalued, ridiculed and discounted — I write this in the hope that she will not be forgotten — just as her house was doomed to be demolished. Yet she had her moment of glory. When the crisis occurred and the whole social structure of the village seemed paralyzed, she emerged with magnificence to suggest that courage and kindness perhaps once existed to a greater degree in our land than we have ever imagined.

I was thirteen that summer and had stopped accompanying my mother to visit Madame Dey. Conformity to social pressures was becoming important, and I was aware that she was regarded as an oddball, an eccentric, a character. One evening in early August when she came to visit us, I remained upstairs in my room reading.

"You hurt Madame Dey by not coming down to speak to her," my mother said afterwards. "She asked me if perhaps you didn't like her coming here anymore."

"She's right," I said sullenly, "None of the other summer people have her to their houses. Why do we have to?"

"You're getting to be the snotty one, aren't you?" my mother retorted. "I'll have ye know that as long as I live she's welcome here, and you'll be civil, or I'll have it out with your father."

The argument turned out to be unnecessary, I am sorry to write. After the tragedy I went back to visiting her and she always greeted me as warmly as ever, but she never came to visit us at home again.

It wasn't much of a tragedy really, so small and inconsequential that it took only four lines in the *Montreal Star* two days later, but it was my first contact with accidental death, and because of Madame Dey, the most dramatic event I have ever experienced.

It was late August, and although the nights came early and were chilly with a touch of fall, the day had been warm and comfortable. We'd changed from our swim and were eating Madame Dey's fresh picked blueberries with warm milk straight from the cow.

We were delighting in the natural milk and berries when we heard a commotion out front. People yelling in French were hustling by the window of our cottage in a state of alarm. My mother went outside to investigate. I put down my spoon and listened. My mother shouted back through the screen door, "There's been a drowning in the lake!"

I ran and joined my mother outside. We scanned the water; a large number of rowboats were at the far point along the railway track.

At the main wharf we could see that a crowd had gathered, awaiting the return of the boats. More people passed on the road, including the King, who stopped to inform us of what he knew.

The drowned man was a stranger. He had arrived by train only that noon, told the hotel he wanted to go out on the lake before lunch and had taken out a rowboat. When he didn't return, the hotelkeeper sent out his son who found the boat up at the point, empty except for a towel, wallet and wristwatch.

Lac Mercier was typically Laurentian in that one can usually judge the slope beneath the water by the slope of the
mountainside at the edge. The drowning occurred at the little sandy strip that belonged to the railway and was considered "public." People went to it by boat or by walking up
the tracks. Although it was a popular place to swim, it was
also considered dangerous. The sandy bottom stretched out
to a depth of four or five feet, then dropped sharply, exactly
where a person wading would not be able to see the bottom
and would assume the gradualness to continue.

"We'll go see Madame Dey," my mother said. "She'll know
all about it."

When we arrived at Madame Dey's, her daughter told us
that she was at the station. There was a crowd on the platform; we went down to find Madame Dey arguing with the
stationmaster. She stopped to explain to us that the hotel
had refused to take the body in; the dead man's parents had
been telephoned in Montreal and were coming up on the
evening train. "They can't leave the boy like that for his
parents to come and find," Madame Dey complained.

A few feet away the crowd parted and we saw what she
meant. The body lay naked, except for swimming trunks,
on the metal wagon used to transport suitcases. We gasped.
The death pangs were still evident in the staring eyes and

distorted mouth, the horror seemingly magnified by the brutal way the iron of the wagon pressed against his flesh.

The crowd, feeling helpless and uncertain, questioned each other: "Why was the man just left there? … Why wouldn't the hotel take him in? … Had Monsieur le Curé been told? …Couldn't Monsieur le Curé speak to the hotelkeeper? … Has anyone told Monsieur le Curé? …Where's Monsieur le Curé? … *Oû est Monsieur le Curé?*" Someone had been to tell the curé, it seemed, but the curé never appeared.

Spotting the King at the far end of the crowd, we went over to him. He stood apart, surveying the scene, his thumbs under his suspenders.

"The hotel won't take the body in," my mother informed him.

"His relatives can sue them for that," the King commented, his left hand gently massaging his stomach.

"Maybe if you were to go to the hotel and tell them that—" my mother said tentatively.

The King shrugged: "It's no affair of mine." Then he added, "I don't see why they're all in such a hurry to get going into the lake. I've lived here well-on twenty years and I never *knowed* the need."

We went back to where Madame Dey was standing beside the stationmaster; my mother reported the King's comment about the hotel being liable. The stationmaster, a mild man who had been transferred to the village only that year, looked uncomfortable. Why should he be burdened with something no one else wanted? The body couldn't be there on the platform when the train arrived. Finally, in desperation, he picked up the handles to the wagon, pushed it into the baggage room, slid the door shut, locked it, and told everyone to go away.

We walked with Madame Dey slowly back up the hill to her house. Madame Dey kept repeating over and over, "They can't leave the boy like that for his parents to come and find." Reaching the door to her house, she stopped suddenly. "I'm going to bring him here," she announced.

"You're not!" my mother said, aghast. "You're not going to bring a dead body into your own house!"

"I am," she said, and we followed her back to the station, hypnotized by her plan.

"Take it if you want it," the stationmaster shrugged. He unlocked and opened the baggage room door and went back to his office. Madame Dey looked at the dead man, put out her hand, and forced his eyes shut. Then, lifting the handles to the wagon, she pushed it outside.

The stationmaster reappeared on the platform. The wagon belonged to the railway company. He could not allow it off railway property. Madame Dey looked at him as if she wanted to memorize his face, then she bent over and raised the body onto her shoulders.

"You can't," my mother protested, close to hysteria. "It's too heavy."

"Go home, go home, I'm all right," she replied, and we just watched, transfixed.

Staggering under the weight, she moved slowly, the head and arms of the dead man flopping terribly down her back. The crowd regathered; cars passing on the road stopped; but no one moved to help her. When at last she reached her front door, a sigh of relief seemed to go up.

We walked back home in stunned silence. For once my mother didn't try to sum things up.

We sat on the sofa in the cottage, staring at the floorboards until darkness fell, then turned and gazed out the window at the lights flickering on across the lake. We could think of nothing but Madame Dey. My mother was shaken. Coming from Ireland, a land of myth and legend, she held any number of superstitions. The idea of bringing the dead body of a stranger into your own house was beyond her.

Suddenly my mother broke the silence. "I want to go back. Will you come with me?"

The door stood open at Madame Dey's house as we walked up the path. Inside, the room where she did her ironing had been transformed. A white sheet covered the table, and the dead man lay stretched upon it, fully dressed. I remember noticing, the way one notices details in frightening moments, the flawless crease in his trousers and the shine on his black shoes. His arms were folded across his chest, his mouth was closed and he looked rather handsome and quite young. At his head stood two tall brass candlesticks, their light putting the rest of the room in shadows. All the furniture had been removed except the kitchen chairs, which were lined up neatly along the far wall, and a small table which held a vase with a single sunflower picked from her garden.

Madame Dey smiled at us slightly as we entered. With a shawl over her head, she looked like a great mourning widow.

The hotel had not wanted to give her the dead man's clothes, but she told them what the King said, that they could be sued for not taking the body in, and threatened to tell the young man's parents to do it unless the hotel handed the clothing over. She had ironed his suit and polished his shoes before starting to dress him; only his shirt had presented a special problem. He had only the one he wore from the city and it was soiled, so she had to wash it and iron it dry, an exasperatingly slow job when there was so much to do.

As for the candlesticks, she had sent her daughter to Monsieur le Curé to get them. "I told her to tell him that if he didn't send me some, I'd go to the church and steal them."

After informing us of how she had accomplished so much, so quickly, Madame Dey announced, "I want to be at the station when the train arrives."

The platform was even more crowded than earlier, for by now the summer people all round the lake had heard the story. An avenue of space and silence opened around Madame Dey as she appeared.

When the great iron engine roared into the station, the ground seemed to shake as if Mont Tremblant itself were trembling. The train slowed, then came to a stop. The crowd shuddered in anticipation as they watched and waited. Then the conductor helped down an unsteady woman with a handkerchief to her face, followed by a bewildered-looking man in city clothes.

Madame Dey walked toward them slowly, as one performing a ceremony. They looked up at her, their eyes helplessly questioning. She bowed slightly and her voice seeming to come from an altar or a mountain as she told them their son was at her home. "*Votre fils est chez-moi. Venez.*"

She pointed to the cottage at the top of the hill beside the church. The front door had been left open and the candlelit room was visible from the platform.

The three figures were silhouetted against the lights from the hotel and general store as they headed up the hill. Madame Dey walked behind as a mother follows an infant up a staircase, ready to give support should it fall back or stumble. They reached the open door: the couple entered and found their son. In the light from inside, we saw the woman's head drop against her husband's shoulder and his arm go around her.

Then Madame Dey entered, and the door was shut against the watching eyes.

That is where I would like to leave this account of Madame Dey, and yet I must, in faithfulness, go to the end. The next summer we arrived by train to find Madame Dey's place, the cottage that had served as a provisional funeral home, gone. The church needed space for a new, expanded sanctuary and Madame Dey's continued presence in the village had begun to take on mythical proportions as the story of her dealing with drowned stranger was told and retold and told again. Madame Dey's rental home was becoming something of an attraction, much to the chagrin of the church next door. These issues were solved when Monsieur le Curé convinced his superiors in Montreal of the need for an expanded sanctuary. He then presented a handsome offer of purchase to the King, who in turn sent it on to the departed chemical company. The sale was made, Madame Dey evicted, and the house levelled.

We found Madame Dey living in a two-room shack a mile south of the village. During the winter, her son Gene had come home from California. He had arrived late in November ill with stomach cancer and died in April. He was forty-two.

The kindness she had shown strangers bereft of a son only the year before was not shown to her. Destitute except for the food and wood sent her by her sons in the village, she had nursed him. "He went away a beautiful young boy, and he came back an old man to die in my arms," she told us.

Madame Dey moved away after that summer. Perhaps she had only stayed on near the village waiting for Gene's return. Did she somehow know he would?

I never saw her again. Our summers at the lake ended. Years later I returned to the village as an adult. I stopped in to see one of Madame Dey's sons, who was doing well as a carpenter now that so many ski chalets were being built. His mother was fine, he told me. She was getting her old age pension, which she had used to help set her son-in-law up in a small business. The city of Montreal had recently outlawed the hot dog and *patate frites* wagons that had been such a happy addition to its streets during my childhood. With her ever-present resourcefulness Madame Dey had managed to buy one, and had moved it just outside the municipal limits.

"But what is she doing with it?" I asked.

"She selling freshly cut French fries. She peels the potatoes by hand."

She peels potatoes! The scene flashed before me like an old film script. How often I'd seen her peel things. Apples, potatoes, anything with a peel. The peel would fall over her wrist in one continuous strip, so thin I would watch spellbound for it to break. It never did until the fruit or vegetable was pared clean. When finally she presented it to me, it no longer seemed like food at all, it was a sculpture, so lovingly had its nature been understood. And the peel would lie coiled on the newspaper at her feet, beautiful as a newly woven ribbon.

———

About the author.

May Cutler (1923-2011) born in Montreal, Quebec, she was founder of Tundra Books in 1967 and the first woman publisher of children's books in Canada. Tundra published the works of artists such as William Kurelek, Ted Harrison, Arthur Shilling, and Song Nan Zhang. May worked with author Roch Carrier and filmmaker Sheldon Cohen to create *The Hockey Sweater*. May was educated at McGill University and Columbia University. She worked for the United Nations before she began a career in journalism, first at the Montreal Herald and later at the Canadian Press. From 1987 to 1991, she served as the first female mayor of Westmount, Quebec. Her childhood memoir, *I Once Knew an Indian Woman* was published in both the Canada and the US. It was awarded first prize in the Canadian Centennial Literary Competition, in 1967 and the *New York Times Book Review* selected it as "an Outstanding Book of the Year" in 1973. The book chronicles her summer's spent at Lac Mercier beside the old village of Mont-Tremblant, Quebec during the 1920s and 30s.May Ebbitt was born in the east end of Montreal in 1923. Her parents, Francis (Farrelly) and William Henry Ebbitt, a police officer, were Irish immigrants. She had two older brothers, William "Bill" Ebbitt and Jack Ebbitt. In 1953 she married Phil Cutler, a Canadian labour lawyer and Quebec Superior Court judge, who died in 1987. The couple had four sons, Keir, Adam and Michael, who are twins, and Roger.

About the editor.

Keir Cutler (playwright and performer) has been performing his solo shows since 1999. He is a veteran of more than 85 fringe festivals and the playwright/performer of 10 original monologues and several plays. He is best known for his award-winning *Teaching Shakespeare* and his adaptation of Mark Twain's *Is Shakespeare Dead?* He has been called "formidably delightful" (Off-Off Broadway Review, NY) "gloriously funny," (Orlando Sentinel), "one hell of a story-teller!" (Vue Weekly, Edmonton), and "a masterful entertainer," (Winnipeg Free Press). Keir is a graduate of McGill University, the National Theatre School of Canada (playwriting), and has a PhD in theatre from Wayne State University in Detroit. Four of his solo shows have been broadcasted on television by BRAVO!/CANADA. Keir has performed at Shakespeare's Globe complex in London, UK before theatrical royalty, Sir Derek Jacobi and Sir Mark Rylance, and at Mark Twain House and Museum in Hartford, Connecticut. In 2019 Keir debuted his monologue based on his mother's work, *I Once Knew an Indian Woman* under the title *Magnificence* directed by Paul Van Dyck. It received rave reviews and was awarded "Best English Text" at the Montreal Fringe Festival.

www.keircutler.com.

www.ingramcontent.com/pod-product-compliance
Lightning Source LLC
Chambersburg PA
CBHW020041040426
42331CB00030B/487